Also by Tayi Tibble

Poūkahangatus

Rangikura

Rangikura

Poems

Tayi Tibble

ALFRED A. KNOPF

New York   2024

Thank you to the editors of publications in which some of the poems
in this book first appeared. "Tohunga" was published in *Literary Hub*
and in *Best New Zealand Poems 2019*, edited by Hera Lindsay Bird.
"That House" was published in *Tales of Two Planets: Stories of Climate
Change and Inequality in a Divided World*, edited by John Freeman
(Penguin Random House, 2020). "Hōmiromiro" was published in
Return Flight: MEL>CHC. 2018 (returnflight.com.au/). "Hine-nui-te-pō"
was published in *Awa Wahine*. "Te Araroa" was published,
in a different form, as "Te Whānau" in *Britomart*.

Library of Congress Cataloging-in-Publication Data
Names: Tibble, Tayi, [date] author.
Title: Rangikura : poems / Tayi Tibble.
Description: New York : Alfred A. Knopf, 2024.
Identifiers: LCCN 2023015484 (print) | LCCN 2023015485 (ebook) |
ISBN 9780593534625 (hardcover) | ISBN 9780593534632 (ebook)
Subjects: LCGFT: Poetry.
Classification: LCC PR9639.4.T45 R36 2023 (print) |
LCC PR9639.4.T45 (ebook) | DDC 821/.92—dc23/eng/20230622
LC record available at https://lccn.loc.gov/2023015484
LC ebook record available at https://lccn.loc.gov/2023015485

Jacket image by Simone Noronha
Jacket design by Linda Huang

Manufactured in Canada
First American Edition

4 the 5024

Honesty, Maturity, Respect

CONTENTS

Tohunga

Visionary like my ancestors I / saw a sky of whales / a pale people /
like my ancestors I / inhaled the bible / swallowed the rifle / like
an 8-inch cock / whateva. / Like Donna Summer I swirled / in a
floor-length dress / said I love to love / I love to fuck / but just like
my ancestors knew / to you I was a savage / wild jasmine / a$$
out / blacked out / with dollar signs / feline like a Bengal tiger and
it's true / that anyone on their hands and knees / is essentially a
praying animal.

Radical like my ancestors I / saw the flower child / the wasted
liberals / and my prehistoric / flare-wearing prince / and like my
ancestors I / kissed and kissed and kissed / and tasted / an entire
lifetime of taking advantage and / being aware of it. / So at least /
when my dress hits the floor / like moulting bark / your eyes follow /
and I can interpret / your fixation as shame. / Are you sorry? / And
what does that say about me / if I think even a suggestion / of an
apology is sexy? So like / my ancestors I / sculpt you from the dirt
until you rise I / make you meet my eye / then suck you all up /
with a slurp like a kina. / That's the way mauri ora. / Just like
Papatūānuku / I breathe life / which is why my mother tongue /
can still sing despite / its history of whippings / I say

good on you babe. / You got what you wanted. / The juicy earth /
the factoried women / the rivers / the mountains / all bowing for
you. / I'm proud of you / the way you erected / monuments in your
image / so foreign so / violently unimagined / just like my ancestors
I / couldn't even have dreamed it. / Pou after pou / of grey and glass /
cracking the sky and the sky / was full of whales. / Wow I say / good
on you babe / then I spread / my hair all over the hotel pillow /
because I love a winner / and you / hit the jackpot with me / with

all us silly girls / for believing you were God / for as long as we did. / But now / the atmosphere is betraying you / and you are reddening in places / where I can bear it. / A warrior / like my ancestors I survived / annihilation. And the awa / that run beneath my skin / have not been lapped dry / just yet / and you can see it all / the unpanned gold / the wild pounamu / the thrashing tuna / family jewels / you can never have / taonga / you can never taste / forbidden fruits / reserved for me / are you afraid again? / like you were of Eve? / The world / is getting unbearably hot / but so am I / and so is she.

Mahuika

Not to be that bitch
but I'm queen of saying things
that I do and don't mean.

I love words so much they blind me.
I'm always speeding
recklessly with star prints burning up
in my irises. I don't mean to
start so many fires
but I've spent my whole life tensing up
waiting for the collision.

I'm the off-cast of half-castes
so I've always had visions
of myself in a thousand pieces.
I'm the off-cast of half-castes
so I've always been comfortable

half-naked and dancing like a flame.
Mahuika giving herself away like
a fatherless bride. Karaka trees
wintering themselves in the moonlight.
Giving it all up for a bots little skux
yeah I love those boys too

and how they always seem to know you
no matter how much ice
the white man tried to baptise you in
and just how cold his gold
chains left you. Actually no.

The river evaporated
at my touch. I was
way too hot. But even so
I'm no Mahuika I'm
Hine-nui-te-pō.
The kind of girl who knows
what's up before the sun slows.

Queen of the club scene grinding
with the gay devils and holding court
with the drag queens. I'm

Hine-nui-te-pō.
The kind of girl who knows
that the real vandalism
happens in the ripeness
of daylight, tagged in

white man's law
and wāhine blood.

So I shrugged fuck it
and learnt to love the dark
where you can either
shine or disappear.

Wear a tacky plastic tiara
4 a heru in my hair. I'm
Hine-nui-te-pō.
The kind of girl who knows

that it's better to make
home in the black

and wait

for all the life that was stolen
from you
to be recycled back.

Can I Still Come Crash at Yours?

We were only girls then iti iti iti but already we were pretty little putiputi growing high amongst the weeds and already we had trained our eyes to pick them out.

You know da ones. Air Force 1s, slacker jeans, jaw of the whale, bandanna bunny tails. We wanted them to pick us too. Spent afternoons in our classrooms praying for them to come thru and satirise themselves. Press their noses against the glass. Make the teacher racist and the eggs laugh. Yeah

we loved those flash hulking diamonds, the best of a bad bunch who, despite the purple fruit punches, the sunny nights, the salt-and-peppered eyes, the police hospitality and the Māori brutality, the AI reality, ripped bodies and ripped copies of Kanye West my bro, my dark twisted fantasy, an iPod with one working headphone, no working dad at home, who were so haati and ngāti, such wholesome wonderful liars, who honestly seemed to glow

like those plastic stick-on stars which in the daylight look like 2-dollar shops and bad taste, but in the dark, on the first beds we ever made for men just like our mothers, shoulder to shoulder beneath their second-hand *Star Wars* covers, palms over their hei matau, they shone almost like the real thing and we were astrologers, drawing dot to dots and making connections where there weren't any. Casting our ships full of wish into the sky.

Our eyes rimmed in raxxed Maybelline would widen and soften and rage and welcome, just like the ocean. We felt watery with understanding that we were yet to understand but we had vague notions, and enjoyed going through the motions of boiling pork bones and vermicelli and braiding or shaving their heads on the stoop during the buzzcut season. Swooping in on their soft babyboi locks 4 matching heart-shaped lockets and our love spells. Chanting

with our hands across our hearts that we did not hope to die but hoped to live, the simple life, of endless American reality TV shows and a couple of chubby kids cos we were down to be wifeys, rolling up and refreshing the ashtrays and the bottles, practised at handling them gently like lovers on a laminated table. So we exchanged vows, not to them but to each other

that every day we would wake up and put our makeup on just to watch them play GTA and exclaim proudly *This is how bad girls do it! From Cape Reinga to the deep blue south!* Marry up and spend our days just swanning on the couch. Real Fitzgerald type shit. Ka mau te wehi. So,

like very good girls we prioritised those boys in their fake Gucci sweatshirts, so genuine, so brainless, we would tell each other we loved them only faintly aware it wasn't true and on the nights we all crashed together marae stylez gazing up at the same stickered roof I turned to you. The empty Tui winding down on the floor, the clock stuck on midnight. Your eyes dilating like big twin moons. I pass you the smoke. You fill up the room.

Lil Mermaidz

Rinsing the sea salt out of our bikinis
with the drinking water and getting a slap
upside the head from your mother with her
House and Garden magazine reserved especially
for fanning away mosquitoes and sighing
because we know that this is how
it's always going to be
because this is how it's always been
because for thirteen years
it seemed that life was nothing but
a succession of hot summers and we were sure
that we were Tangaroa's daughters, the way
we adapted to each turn in the river.

And I remember the year
we were the two strongest "girl swimmers"
in our syndicate. This meant
we were forever forced to race
the boys for Western feminism
and you would always win,
even against the boys who were so like men
the teachers treated them as if they were
more muscle than human.

In the damp parts of afternoons
we'd watch them running laps and
ripping Papatūānuku up
with their cleats. Their teeth clenched
around orange slices of rubber and the reo.
Well I felt sorry for them

slapping kia mate ururoa kei mate wheke
into their chests. Maybe
they wanted to be dolphins instead.

But that was our job, to dive dumb
into the skin of the sea and throw
our heads full of good hair skywards,
saluting the sun. Making scenes
of ourselves when we should have been
slinging pipis into your mother's kete
reserved especially for stealing kai moana.
But I was vegetarian and I didn't wanna
have anything to do with prying kina
loose from the rocks
to offer up to the bros like pussy.
Them slurping and spitting while we flinch
oi don't and they just chur each other on
like a pack of crackling gods.

And I can't remember where we were
but I can guess that we were probably
doing what we were always doing,
during those summers that sweltered
with a swagger, standing on the sand
picking out which surfers we wanted
or tanning on our backs in the soft parts
of the river bank but somewhere
between the boys and the wet
centre of the earth I said Hey
have you ever noticed the way
boys seem to wiri when they're angry?
The way their eyes roll back and
their lips pull tight? That's adrenaline,

you say, taking a thirsty glug of water
you want to bottle it, you say.
100% New Zealand Pure.

Takakino

Cracking like two eggs
in a single bed
playing all
of *Born to Die*
off a fat desktop computer
with no internet.

Making ourselves upset
over the things that make us
girls: Bambi eyes, black bikinis
and all the boys who were either
too skux or too stoned
to text back. Upto next?

Skulled two bottles
of 10-dollar Kristov.
Necked on in the park.
Carked it in a random flat.
Yeah we really showed each other

the tukutuku patterns
on our upper thighs. Cried.
Made a blood pact
with a broken wine bottle
in the gutter.
The most magic and urban
of awa.

I cut her
like a master carver.

I was forever
treating her
like she was a precious piece
of rimu but

blunt and waka blonde
she cut a little too deep
and nearly comatose and rolling
I lolled and lolled and lolled and nearly
bled out on the street. Wobbling

like an oasis. The lights had us
blinking like shot does.
When we got stopped by the cops
well that was so hot.
I loved everything about it
the certain way she made everything
feel fictional and lowkey
that's still my favourite way to feel.

Where are you two girls going?
On our way home poaka!
If home meant wherever
we could get in.
In the random bathtub
we woke up in actually

that was the worst night of my life.
The specific way
my mother looked at me in the morning
with all the mauri evaporating
from her eyes I couldn't even cry
but it changed me.

How did it change you?

And tbh the glitter
of broken cars on lawns and
tagged-up playgrounds
were losing their lustre anyway
and my lust for it.

For a while
it seemed like everything
we touched
seemed to erode a little.

We knew it and yet
it still hurt
to be called destructive.

Each time we reached out,
our fingers stained green
with cheap, stolen rings,
the whole world recoiled.

It was hard to be good.
It was hard to be loyal.

Homewrecker

When I was a girl
God tested me with stepbrothers.
I was eight years old.
I was thirteen.

They were mean.
I began to nurse a few
feminist embers
that they were happy to fan

with their grandmother's
leaf-shaped ili slapped
on the back of my head or
the whip of wet tea towels
exposing the white in my legs.
I wondered if it was true
that you can grow too used to
the feeling of pink pain spraying?

On a good day
you might have called them spirited
the same way Satan is spirited,
all cigarette butts and stink bombs.
I was offended by the audacity
bleaching their bright Samoan smiles. Well,

I was soulful. Only used to
baby-soft sisters and playing the piano
and it physically hurt me.
Every wince seemed to shuck

my ribs from my spine as I witnessed them
pulling electronics apart like a carcass,
searching for the static in the back of the stereo.

Then one Christmas an uncle
whose actual relationship to anyone
we couldn't quite place
gave the younger one
a mechanical Beavis or Butt-Head
I dunno which one
but you'd press the button
on his plasticated stomach
and he would say something
rude and crass and gross
but ultimately forgettable.

He unwrapped it,
studied it.
It seemed like for once
in his little brutal life
he was actually considering
his words, choosing tenderly
until finally he gave his reply
and his reply was
Should I break it?

And we all sighed and rolled our eyes
with the distinct feeling that life
was suspiciously too predictable
and already we knew everything
that we would ever be doing.
Well, I didn't grow up wrecking things
but very often

the world wrecked itself around me.

Even if I was light
on the kitchen floorboards
the geraniums curtseyed,
fish threw themselves
from their fishbowls,
punks crumpled
on their skateboards
and I always won Jenga.

Even my mother said I had a talent
for extracting things from people
and so I had to be careful.
No one was going to light up
violently and tell me
that I was taking something from them.
Life's not a game of Operation.
Stop playing with people.
But I'm lonely Mum. I'm a Libra
I'm a Libra just like you.

As a teenager,
a man whose opinion I truly trusted
said I was a dangerous girl
and this made me so afraid of myself.
I avoided being alone with her.
I never left her unattended.
I made sure she had someone
with her at all times.
Even if they belonged
to someone else, they were mine.

And pink pain became desirable.
As an adult, the sensation
found a home in my chest.
It reminded me of tea towels
and hidings and how
fresh to death and nervous
but alert, and alive I was then.

I can't remember the last time
I ever saw my brothers but I recall

Playing Jenga
and how long it would take
to stack the blocks
perfectly
only to take turns
trying to take
without destroying.
Which is where I learnt
to understand the risk
and do it anyway.
I just hold my breath.
Wait.

That House

In that house I lived in a pink lavalava.
Watched *Lilo & Stitch* with my sister
at least three times a day.
Delivered kittens in the kitchen and gave them away
to neighbours knowing too well
that *Ohana means family*
and family means nobody gets left behind
even if you want to be forgotten.
Something or someone always finds its way back
scratching at the screen door.

And in that house with the screen door
I showered with my underwear still on.
Played piano wet and limply
with my eyes closed. Escaping
up the tree to read all seven of
the Chronicles of Narnia until I fell
asleep and every morning
the sun was as bright and as startling as birth.
I developed an early kind of kinship
with all the ways the earth hurt.
With a toy stethoscope and that lavalava
I nursed wounds that made me wobbly
and only half visible, like a mirage.

And in that house with the piano
my mother was a mirror.
Pretty for as long as she could
hold herself together.
We wanted to stare but were afraid

that the pressure would cause cracks.
Couldn't tell if she would harden
like a diamond or collapse like sand.
The moon was in Capricorn and the man

of the house was busy shucking anything
he could get at with his machete.
Sundays were punctuated
by the hack hack hack and the nervous
rustling of bibles. Everybody knew
what was happening and prayed silently
like good disciples. No altars,
no candles, no fireplace

in that house so the wood
was stacked for the sake of
creating something looming.
As if a butterfly kiss might send
the entire thing tumbling. So we spent
whole seasons waiting with our breath
dissipating on the insides of our mouths
while he was out there
huffing and puffing on whatever
he could puncture with his teeth.

And in that house with no heat
I believed in the cold.
Thought I would grow old
like the piano and have to watch
that video forever.
But even winter eventually
weathers itself and when
the number was finally called

it was spring
and the sprockets of blue and purple
were blooming too brightly
to politely ignore.

Mars in Scorpio

In the winter
when we first got together
I had just bought a pink houndstooth coat
with my power bill money.

We rolled
20-dollar notes
between our fingers and bumped
until our lips hummed.
Did it hurt?
I can't remember it
hurting. All I recall is studying
the crushed city with
the hungriest of eyes
and it was pretty.
Far prettier than me, or you.

He was new for me.
You wouldn't have recognised him.
I was the animal
baiting the animal out of him.
I read too many poems
exactly like this one
and sent them over text
like nudes, like ekphrasis
in reverse. We never knew
who was responding to who.

But he was new. Brand new.
Even his bad news was good.

I could wait
entire days and nights
for those three grey dots
to appear like the oracles.

He'd pour
tea cups of thick wine
we'd never finish
each night and each morning
after he'd been busy
breaking not my heart but maybe
the bars around it he would pluck
an apple out of thin air
and present it to me
as if I was the teacher
and he was the pet
so there was nothing to do
but roll my eyes
give them a good wipe and say
thank you.

Thank you.

So I ate with my eyes closed
thinking I enjoyed
the sound of smacking.
The wet crunching,
like bones at the bottom
of the ocean.
I thought to myself
Just like a pearl
I have been smoothed by friction.
Underwater volcanoes.

Bubbling. Simmering.
I thought to myself
I am the type of girl
who can withstand such tension.

I recognised that
the East Coast girl in me
has always been
waiting for a natural eruption.

And in the aftermath,
I saved my coat from the floor

so on the nights when I was powerless
I held it to myself.
I was snuffing out a flame.

He might have been the same
for you but he was new
for me. I told him
as seriously as I could,
my eyes solemn
like black water, that

I desire mystery.

There were many things
I did not want to know about.
You especially.

Hot Hine Summer

4 the skux I bought fresh sneakers every month.
Let my hair curl real trip hop. Fed my ass fat
with slutty foods: pineapple and cranberry juice.

Still down for a feed tho! Proud of how cute I can act while
splitting a bucket. Because Gigi and Bella Hadid pretending
to eat In-N-Out Burger in California blue convertibles

is big dick energy and I'm happy committing to the image
that I'm always finger lickin' good. So I got my nails done
in the colour True Kardashian Neutral. Smoked up

until I was chill chill chill and basically brain dead. Left him
on read. Played too hard to get but too hot to leave until
I copped that CCV code like a bad bitch. Placed orders

for obsolete things like Fashion Nova skinny tea and waist trainers
in the hopes that he might lick my blunt with his pūkana and step
dreamers out like a nightmare and then betray me

with a white bitch so white hot that nobody talks about the fact
that she wears foundation a whole colour wheel darker.
Doesn't matter. There's still plenty of fish and lizards and

demigods to crush between my thighs and at least
with my indigenous sunkiss and foreign shapewear
I still look well-sculpted like Hineahuone so

4 the daddy I demanded fresh frangipanis every month.
Learned to hot-roll my hair real paradise edition.
Wore ridiculous lingerie sets with serious conviction.

Considered taking up cigarettes for a proper vintage look.
Practised making significant eyes in the mirror.
More honey, come and hither and less kapa haka.

I read poetry in public places and kept
paperbacks in my Prada only to use them like fans
to accessorise my Antoinette-style heaving.

And in the evenings I tore at steaks with all my bad teeth and
I cannot stress this enough it was extremely fashion forward.
Whole civilisations applauded.

I latched on to this and developed a taste for elaborate cocktail
umbrellas. Hoarded invitations to swanky lobotomies
where I sipped Dom Perignon and rolled my eyes in divination.

Had revelations that the future is essentially a hundred dollar bills
in a tight white fist exploding against the automatic ass of an AI stripper.
Yes, even the robots will be programmed with excessive desire.

Well, what did you expect? It's the 20s again and all I wanted,
like Daisy Buchanan, like a beautiful fool, was him
to fly me out and put me up in a bougie as mansion then go die in the pool.

4 the atua I asked for fresh forgiveness every month.
Let my hair curl real East Coast like all furls
of the whenua. Got my reggae on

to *Rua Kēnana* and chanted
Tūhoe prophet of Te Urewera
every weekend, in a garage, like a ritual.

Started wearing my lipstick on my chin
and the places I thought
were too fat I now thought were too thin.

I ate off the land. I lived by the moon because
that's where I thought I'd see him down by the river,
eel fishing by spotlight while I was out here having my

monthly hallucinations, bleeding
into the whenua, paling holographic,
waiting for him to appear.

And in the coldest parts of nights like this
when my body was nothing
but a hot summer making the water

steam and levitate towards the sky it was clear
that even God was ghosting
my messages, my prayers.

And I thought of Mary Magdalene, her beautiful hair
and how degraded she must have felt. Doesn't matter
that it was Jesus. All men think they're God's gift.

Hōmiromiro

I used to dream
about a two-headed goldfish.
I took it for an omen.
I smashed a milk bottle open

on a boiling road and watched
a three-legged dog lick it up
and in the process I became
not myself but a single shard
of glass and thought finally

I had starved myself skinny enough
to slip into the splits of the universe
but once I did I realised that the universe
was no place for a young thing to be
and there is always a lot more starving to be had.

When I was a girl I thought

I was Daisy Buchanan.
I read on the train.
I made voluminous eyes.

Once I walked in front of a bus and it exploded
into a million monarch butterflies
then I was ecstatic!

As a girl, I could only fathom

time as rose petals falling
down my oesophagus.
It tickled and it frightened me.
I ran around choking for attention.

I had projections of myself
at 100
my neck weathered and adorned
like the boards of a home
being eaten by the earth.

When I was a girl I would lie

on the side of that road
in the last lick of sun and wait
for the rabbits to come saluting
the sky of orange dust

and then I would shoot them into outer space.

For many years I watched them
bouncing on the moon.
But then I stopped caring and so
I stopped looking.

Little

She wears white on whites with her tennis skirt, not the pumps that lift her ass into a love heart, but he is too disinterested with hangover to go for a walk anyway, even though it was his idea. Instead, they watch music videos on the hotel television. She says she likes production that is shiny like lamé. He says her taste is mindless. She holds her breath while a tacky song plays and only exhales when he raises an eyebrow, acknowledging the embarrassing lyrics. I want you to ruin my life. Jesus, he says, mimicking alarm but genuinely laughing. She laughs too and feels like she might have some love for him, but only while the song plays.

2

Afterwards, he takes her to a Chinese restaurant. He uses a fork so she uses a fork. She spears a piece of Kung Pao chicken. About halfway through her dish she realises that the staff are watching her. Their eyes blink red like security cameras. She can taste the bowl she smoked by the scent in her hair and she tells herself that she is being paranoid but when she meets their eyes directly they do not look away. So she looks away. She looks back again. She looks at her plate, rice, peanuts and meat, and looks back again. They are staring harder somehow. For fuck's sake, she thinks. She drops her fork and widens her eyes as if to bark *What*. Her tongue feels like a wild eel inside her mouth. She considers poking it out but decides against it and sighs. One of them is young but older than her. He is thin and wearing a soggy cap. He is straining so intensely to stare that the bones and sinew in his neck are standing to attention. He looks like a chicken preparing his own neck for the cleaver. She puts her fork down. The chicken man leans forward and knocks the Eftpos machine off the counter. The clang on the linoleum is a physical pain, but no one else in the restaurant seems to notice. She looks at him shovelling food off his plate, and wishes they could swap seats. What's this dish called again? he asks her for the third time. I should be the one showing you new things, he says, shaking his head. After dinner, he tells her that he needs to make a phone call. He tells her to walk back in front of him.

3

Back at the hotel he makes a big show of still being sick from big nights, then he turns his back and goes to sleep at ten. She calculates that she is on two or three hours' sleep. She feels deeply exhausted yet buzzy and electrical, like a little robot. Actually, she decides, she is deeply bored. She tries to cry a little but no tears come. She tries to go to sleep but she's disturbed by the cold. His body, she realises, doesn't give off a lot of heat. She transforms into a cat, and mews, and makes pirouettes and paws him. In the morning he teases her. He tells her that she is embarrassing but with a smile. And anyway he rolls over and makes room for her.

4

Despite her protests he makes her go to work for a few hours. She meets him in the afternoon in a different hotel lobby. He is drinking tea and swallowing painkillers. She drinks two glasses of rosé and becomes funny. A phone call steals fifteen minutes, which seems greedy but she tries her best not to feel jealous or think bad thoughts. His car arrives before she is prepared for it. He asks her if she wants a lift back to work on the way. She doesn't want to go back to work but she says okay. In the back seat she notices the warmth her body releases. She draws a tiny heart in the heat on the window, then promptly crosses it out. She meets eyes with the driver in the rearview mirror. The driver parks and he says bye now. She gets out of the taxi and wills him to look back but he doesn't, like Lot. She tastes salt in the corners of her mouth. Her chest hardens.

5

He tells her he will text her from the plane but he doesn't. On the way home she buys a jumbo bag of M&Ms. When she gets home she doesn't open them, she just feels stupid and lies on her bed. She wakes up with her shoes and the lights still on. On the way to work, she throws the M&Ms in someone's recycling bin. After work she takes a walk, near the water, in the sun, with her headphones in. That night she spends over 200 dollars on cocktails and stays out until 3am. A DJ DMs her on Instagram and they meet, both very drunk, outside her favourite club on the street. The club has closed down now, and its boarded-up windows give her a quiet throb of grief. The DJ is tall and forward and physical, but she gets in her Uber alone anyway. The DJ was only in town for one night. She wakes up to a text the next day. *I hope you are alone.*

6

She begins waiting at 9am. At 9am either his house has emptied or he has left for work. 10am and no word, so she makes herself something slutty to eat—canned pineapple and sliced strawberries in a white bowl. At 11am she works a little. At 12pm she daydreams and adds an expensive pair of shoes to her cart before closing the browser. At 1:23pm he calls but not for long. He says he will text her soon, but he only sends two more texts then stops replying. She skips the party she said she would go to and stays in bed watching recommended videos on YouTube. She orders an expensive pizza and only eats the mushrooms off. She pays $17.99 for a book he mentioned in passing and skim-reads approximately a third of it on her Kindle until she falls asleep. She wakes up with the light still on. She gets up and turns it off. She can't fall asleep again. The sun starts coming up. Her room fills with light blue, and light blue, and light blue.

7

At work she goes outside to the car park to read a book in the sun. She sits where she always sits, on a ridge of concrete between two parked cars. The Chinese restaurant on the floor below her fills the air with the thick smell of grease, but she is used to it now. For 30 minutes she doesn't look at her phone. The sky is light blue.

8

A man she had a week-long fling with is back in the country. She had liked him. He took her out for cocktails five nights in a row. He gave her $1000 in an orange envelope so she could go shopping. With the money she bought three sets of lingerie, three pairs of earrings, a pink tweed skirt, a fake plant, a box of macaroons and two bottles of Chilean wine. He wants to take her out, so she lets him and wears the pink set, not the black. Black, they agree, is the best colour. It's just one of the many things they have in common. The man asks her what she has been reading lately and she says nothing. He frowns and she looks out the window. The sky is light blue.

9

She does not hear from him for many days, long enough for the expectation that he will text her to change into the expectation that he won't.

10

On a Sunday night she gets a call at ten. She stares at his emoji on her home screen in soft disbelief. The last time he phoned her this late he was standing in the middle of the street, describing the poplar trees before whispering that work was sending him to her city that weekend. She stares at his emoji. She stares at his emoji. She believes it will disappear. She picks up and her breath goes ha and low.

11

She is nervous. She applies her makeup carefully. She dresses modestly. She has trouble fixing the button at the back of her blouse so she leaves it. When she steps out of her apartment lobby she feels the cold exaggerate in goosebumps on her neck. In the lift up to his room she has the sickening feeling of stage fright and has to move from elevator to room number and force herself to knock faster than she can convince herself to turn around and abandon this. He answers and smiles at her in a way that reminds her of kettle popcorn. She is softened by the sense she always gets—that he takes so much pleasure in looking at her. His eyes swallow. Her chest swells. She feels proud of him, for being good like that.

12

Immediately, without a word, he undresses her, then himself, and pours into her. She feels as if she is absorbing his entire mass. A meaningless thought occurs to her. We are joined in a very dark way, she thinks. She goes to the bathroom. When she returns he is sitting on the edge of the bed, running his hands through his hair. Poor baby, she thinks suddenly, and a surge of something forces herself onto his lap. He holds her, but without commitment. She has to strain her abs and monkey her arms around his neck to keep balance. She tries to kiss his mouth but misses. I'm going to get a lot of bad karma for this, he tells her. He won't look at her. She takes his face in her hands and sours her nose. Hey hey hey, she coos as if speaking to a baby. Hey hey hey hey hey. Maybe I am good karma. You know? A reward for something you have done in your life. Oh baby, he says. His arms steel up around her. Oh baby baby baby baby baby. He brushes hair off her face. I've never done anything good in my entire lifespan. Not once. Not even a little.

13

She spends more time in his city, coincidentally. She tries not to have expectations but finds herself having expectations, which sometimes he meets and exceeds with an effortlessness that leaves her breathless. Other times she is left underwhelmed and winded. She finds herself alone, on some spoiled sheet, feeling like a scribble. Sometimes his visits are so brief, arriving so late and leaving so early, that they make no impression on her body. She wakes in the exact same position she was dozing in before his call, and it's like they were never there, like nothing ever happened at all.

14

Still, she likes it best when he takes her out for dinner. She doesn't mind that the places are ugly and out of the way. They agree that these types of places have their charms. It's just one of the many things they have in common. Their dish isn't on the menu so he orders a shrimp dish and she orders some vegetables so they can share, although she never eats off his plate and he never notices. He excuses himself. He strokes her face as he leaves. She sips her lemon lime and bitters and tries to make out what a painting across the room might be depicting. After a great deal of thought she concludes that it is some sort of mythical bird that represents death. While he is absent, the woman at the table over leans over to speak to her. She can tell, not even by her expression, but from the air of haughty tension around her that what she is about to say is unpleasant. What would your father think? Ashamed, ashamed. Her voice is low and rushed as if she is the one who is ashamed. Her face is fat and red and wobbles like a flame. Later that night, when she is full and happy, his heavy head resting on her belly, meaningless thoughts occur to her about being shamed before she was born, before she even had the chance to do anything wrong. She thought he was sleeping, but she feels his consciousness against her skin. He wants to do something wrong again.

15

There are gifts too: apples and plums, a fresh tube of cool mint tooth-paste, a plastic ring in a plastic bauble, the wrong-coloured lipstick from Yves Saint Laurent, a paperback biography of a sexually deviant writer, a tiny brown monkey that wraps around a pencil, a bottle of wine from 2003, a white teddy, a tiny skirt, earrings which on second thought look too mature, some spindly flowers from his garden, the choice between a Bounty and a Milkybar. Thank you, she says, I like coconut. He grins and says, I thought you might. He is much more of a Milky Bar anyway. But it is his joke, not hers.

16

Yet another weekend. She feels plump like a pig with good fortune. He spoils her. Both nights he takes her to the same Spanish restaurant, which surprises her, because the restaurant is fashionable and popular. He is, for the most part, a creature of habit, but on the second night she asks him to break it so they can sit at the table by the window. She looks down onto the main road and watches girls both as over- and under-dressed as she is laughing and drawing attention to themselves. She is dreaming when she kicks his leg under the table. Sorry she says, but he just smiles and catches her heel in one hand, accidentally spilling his Corona with the other.

17

The next day is hard before there is even daylight. It's often like this. She lies in the dark, one hand over her heart, and the other clasped over her mouth. She is annoyed with herself. She is in pain. When the time comes he helps with her suitcase, bougie, but one of the wheels is crushed lower than the others. He is good like that. She orders her ride to arrive round the back. They wait. She turns to face him, but bows her forehead into his chest instead. When she arrives back to her apartment, she is confronted with the fact she left clothes all over her bed. She scrapes them into a pile on one side, gets underneath her covers and leans into the clothes pile. She is falling asleep, unravelling, thinking of tiny holographic celebrities, embarrassing poetry, futuristic surveillance, metropolitan igloos, bible verses, being in a club and being served a cocktail made of M&Ms and seawater, then crying to an AI DJ *That's not my drink*, the pile of books by her bed, oil spills and factory smog, chocolate bars and fake plants, poplars, popcorn, paper, plastic baubles, hundreds of them, a phoenix painting the sky Chinese restaurant red, her room filling light blue again. When she dreams she hears her phone singing, the sound tacky, bright and mindless.

Kehua / I used to want to be the bait that caught Te Ika

I lost my nerve for spirits when I was sixteen. Spent that whole spring playing chicken and betraying my grandparents' liquor cabinets for homies who were too cool to say thank you but the slight acknowledgement, sunrise in their chin, suggesting warm and wicked days, eyes lighting up the colour of blunts, bark and honey, was enough to make me feel like Māui, full of confidence and concoctions, under pressure to slow the sun.

So I was like fuck it lesh go and have some fun. I'd smuggle our mixes onto the 11:40 train in Pump bottles and V cans, offering sips to pigs and the random neon vests that looked after the station post the jumpings. Why me? Because none of my friends knew how to play poker properly and this was annoying, after I spent that whole winter playing Texas hold 'em on the Xbox that my stepdad swapped the dog for.

And then there was the midnight game. 1am or so. Only the insane girls would play. AKA hunt or be hunted. When the whole suburb collapsed from the hustle and the grind, settled into a lullaby of weed, wine and infomercials, that's when we'd rise, in our little white SaveMart nighties, chuck on our big black Docs and go round the streets pulling down cars, not on purpose but just by pull. In those days, the stars were as ugly as piercings in the sky and I didn't know what the hell the planets were up to. I thought I might be a child of the moon but as it turns out I'm Venus ruled, and I give off a hot pink glow.

Sometimes the air was so charged I thought it might snow. We'd shiver like apparitions, all the bass leaking out of us, as cars of the most glamorous cliché, heavy set Subarus and neon-green Nissans with spoilers like scorpions would pull up and, recognising the angel in us, would ask us, how long have you been here circling the circumference of the sun?

Sometimes we'd lie a little. Sometimes the truth was more fun. Either way, their reactions were always engineered and the same, and this interested me, as if everything was a rehearsal and time was a scratched CD that needed to be thumped and skipped back, over and over again. They'd say pretty, fucking and young. Adjust their caps. Pinch the bridge of their nose. Orchestrate a big scene of cinematic hesitation, then ask us to get in their car. Where? I dunno. Just a cruise. There's nowhere to go round here anyway, and we all knew it, and loved it, and were bored, and abused it.

Sometimes there would be VBs, Tuis, half a soggy joint, a tiny fairy on a tiny tab of card, a tattooed hand, an astringent jaw, and in the midst of keeping track of these things we'd see them, so fiercely bright they'd stick in our eyes and make us cry. That's when we'd know to push ourselves out of the passenger's seat and run like doe and gunshot.

Was it ritualistic? Yes it was ritualistic. And yes, I used to want to be the bait that fished up Te Ika. But Nana kissed my face over and over after her funeral and said shh bubba shh. And these days I don't have to summon anything so brutally anymore. The sun rises and sets and I try to take notice of it when I can. The urge to be a passenger in a vehicle going so fast that the soul leaves the body and the mind is wiped clean – I rarely feel it anymore but if I did I would only have to think about phrenologists, supernatural science, and all the nerves and notifications in my body that have kept the animal in me alive this far, and feel glad that I don't have to kill a rabbit to know it has a heart.

Hine-nui-te-pō

Half-caste daughters
of half-castes
about to fall into quarters.

Cast out into cities
and universities
and forgotten about.

Their umbilical cords cut
and dumped in a sludge
of hospital waste.

The lobotomised smiles
on their faces while bumping
a line off the back of

a phrenology textbook.
Shook at all the colours
you can find in a skull.

Taking boyfriends
like appointments with a doctor.
A finger in the mouth and

wanting to say
ah or amen
or ugh, men.

The migraines.
The light coming in.
The inherited trauma of

deeply existing in the space of
separated parents.
The long nights and the

sleep paralysis. Lying
on your back and pushing
the sky from your chest

with thighs that kill demigods.
The violence of divorce, the space
it leaves. The shock of the light

coming in. The distance.
The difference between
heaven and the knowledge

that your first mother was hell
and chose to be.
Reconciling

what it means to be her daughter.
Getting her magic bible bashed
out of you. Running away to

cities and universities downloading
Tinder and getting assimilated in
white minimalist bedrooms.

Imported plants from Bunnings
overgrowing and infecting the whenua.
When it was my turn to come clean I said

I grew up tacky and hungry and dazzling.
I grew up neck-deep in the dirt
but all I needed was a good pair of eyes

to see the stars first
which meant I got a lot of wishes.
But I only had one thing to wish for.

All my fathers are in the sky anyway
I know I don't have to say it
but Mum you should have tied me

to the ground.
Instead I was given
to this city freely.

Friends on benes.
Crown apologies.
Wannabe it-girls at parties.

I wonder how it feels
to be tethered somewhere
by a sense of home. To be buried

in your urupā and to find that when you die
you have been waiting
for yourself, this whole time, all along.

Te Araroa

It was a tweet, a tohunga dream, a tohu
in the sky, that told me my iwi would be
guarding their tribal lines and despite
having only looked my maunga in the eye
once, slept only a handful of nights
beneath the spine of my tipuna, I felt
isolation. Real isolation. The feeling of falling
and having the wind knocked out of you.

This is what I remember.

Rising before daylight but wishing it away.
The sun coming up and the lid going on.
Uncles fucking up the reo they spent ages scraping
together. The heartbreaking habit of looking for her
laughing somewhere along the newspapered table.
Driving away, and in the rear-view mirror watching
my whole heart disappear into the whenua she grew up on.
No. That she grew up *with*. Not on.

Afterwards, my uncles and cousins made forts
of driftwood on the shore. I walked by myself
through the town – a hall and a Four Square –
to a paddock of staunch horses waiting for their kids
like school buses and felt overwhelmed.

Overwhelmed by the land and the ocean
as far and wide and dramatic and endless as the mind
could even try to hold it.

I imagined living like this: all sea and no obstruction.

As I stood with the Pacific all up in my pupils and the breath
of Whetumatarau, mourning against my neck, and felt isolation.
Real isolation. As cold and as brilliant as gunmetal.

When I was little
my mother would tell me a story
about the people we were once and how,
when the muscle from the north moved in
with its mechanical arms of settler fire,
we moved up into the motherhood of our maunga.
For months and months and months.
But when the land was plucked over
and her teat sucked to powder,
the hunger came with a violence so violent
that we traded and ate our children.
Auē Auē Auē.
God forgive me for
I used to be so ashamed.

When I was little I cried
in front of sixty alien eyes
because my teacher

told the entire class
that the Māori killed the moas,
then let them boo me.

Now I think, fuck the moas.
Up to 10 feet tall and an ostrich
is freaky enough. What's the bet
they could rip even our most
#savage Rangatira apart?
But you never see Pākehā
on the internet typing
moa's killed the maoris

My killa lives in the other city.
Said goodbye with an Uber to the airport
and a kiss on my skull.
As I tried not to cry into my mask
I was reminded of the first time
I casually tried to slip some feelings in a text
and he sent back a weak chain of xxxx's.
God I was embarrassed.
Embarrassed that I could feel each x
like tukutuku beneath my skin,
like cuts and crops and kisses and targets.
I was forced to remember that,
wherever I go,
even if I go nowhere at all,
I am still a descendent of mountains
and they are still beautiful despite
everything they've entertained.
Despite everything changing around them,

they remain hearty and generous and gorgeous.
And ever since they were first fished up
by Māui—that sexy skux—every day,
they are the first in the world
to feel the sun on their face,
and knowing this helps
the East Coast girl in me to be brave.

I come from a line of wyling women.
Born like Aphrodite in the blood spill
East Coast sea. They teach me
to live life violently.
I've always been the kind of girl
too tough to be touched softly.

I come from a line of blazing women
born in the red mouth of mountains
that first kiss the sun. They teach me
to live life for fun.
I've always been the kind of girl
too fire to be handled with care.

Actually I'm air just like my mother
and I can't be handled at all.

I'm a Libra like my mother.
As a girl she kneeled in a valley
of teal and let a dozen wild horses
stamp a whirlpool around her

while her mother screamed silently
from the balcony then gave up,
and shrugged, and left her to it.

In the car after the river,
Te Kahureremoa said that in some tellings
Tāwhirimātea is actually a girl.
Oh I said, long and slow, understanding that
I understood something that only girls know.
That makes too much sense actually.
The bros raging and impulsive,
creating earthquakes and tsunamis.
Stepping out their father and sending him away.
What's that ancient whakataukī again?
Oh yeah. Boys will be boys.

But my heart goes out like an abandoned swan boat
ghosting along a lake to Tāwhirimātea, begging everyone
to stay safe in the dark love forced upon them. But
when Rangi had enough—his duffel bags in the blue Subaru—
she went with him to the sky, to spend her entire life
delivering his mamae to their mother, like love letters.

In my city
I always forget the wind until I leave it.
Until I swallow
in the window of a foreign city,
and realise that something is missing,
but not what.

My Ancestors Send Me Screenshots

My ancestors send me screenshots of your group chats dissecting me with all the science of your founding fathers and the sympathy of your murdering mothers wanting to know who I am where I've been and who I've been with. What the fuck is a whakapapa? Do I carry it in my pussy? In a tiny baggy? Like a real 1? Like a down-ass bitch? Do I have a heart? And does it bleed? Like a steak? If it's brutalised enough? If it's served? On a plate? With proper silverware? And presented to your queen still beating would she care? Would she believe? Would she collapse into a frothing fit? With the knowledge? Like a prophet? Like the rhythm of waves smashing up the East Coast, and see? That all our cousins are locked up for growing plants on their own whenua. For putting food in the mouths of children. For being the mouths of children. With no homes, not even the bones of homes to return to. Instead, souls get trapped in subdivisions. They mooch around, kick Fletcher cones and let the air sigh out of tyres. Auē. And wait for the next good day when there is no distinction between cement and sky. If you lie starfished at the bottom of this rock, look up and let your eyes go swimming until you realise that you are also in the clouds looking down like a god and I see all. I'm an omniscient woman, just like my women, and my ancestors send me screenshots. And I already know what you think of me. I've known now for centuries.

Yum Yum Noodles (Beef Flavour)

If you want beef then you should know
that we eat a lot of red meat
where I'm from in the stale-yellow
steakhouse with the stepdad with
the short-man complex
who could play anything on anything
& would laugh & call us little bitches
but the laughter was never musical.

Yeah I was raised up with the mongrels (ruh)
but I'd imagine them
in monogrammed Louis Vuitton
like Tinkerbell, & this made me feel
like an heiress whenever I had one
puppyish & in their bag
buying me whatever I want
from the dollar-bags at the dairy.
Stealing *Creme* & *Dolly* magazines
beneath their hoodies for their lil baddie.

Ascot Park Avenue Princess.
That's my 12-year-old trap name.
At school we'd chant *AC Eurrah*
until the blood
in our cheeks turned blue.

& the quad was a mutherfukn zoo.
If you made eyes you better be able to throw down.
Haka could be heard from the other side of town.
We'd pull up with our pride to the train station

& stamp maroon uniforms into the concrete.
One day a kid showed up with a meat cleaver
& we were all like aye wtf boi?
But then we were all like hey give us a turn too
oi and yeah
he was from Tūhoe,
had that hearty-dark
Scorpio thing about him
but I'm not traumatised. I'm tender.

Yeah everyone wanted to be hard
but the worst thing you could be
was a blender.
No blenders,
we'd repeat like parlay,
like pirate law,
keen to make each other
outlaws,
mean girls,
you can't sit with us
& watch with
crackling Coca-Cola laughs
as the lames limped away dragging their
big broken tails
across the schoolyard.

But it wasn't all hard.
There were parts I loved
like sharing headphones
on the bus listening
to Lil' Kim.
Then all of us
the whole bus

suddenly busting out with
Keep it G,
look out for my peeps!
& knowing it was true
& we would always do our best
to spread luv and feed each other
keep coming thru
with the hookups.

Hungover at the markets
a packet of 10 wet
meat kebabs & panikeke
to share. Chop suey
& chow mein
thick in the air.
The understanding
that everything
tastes better
wrapped in a leaf
& you better enjoy it,
because we all knew
eating good like this
is rare.

Cos where I come from
we know
scabbing
1-dollar chips
Nesian 101
if you don't walk it off
it goes straight to your hips
& I can still wobble
with that p-town swagger

& I still can feel
that anger & that hunger
& I'm not making
any more metaphors here but

don't you worry about me
because I'm good sis I'm full &
I don't want no beef but

if you bring it to my table
everybody gonna eat.

4 the Dead Homies

We cut watermelons on the doorstep while the uncles were smoking imported cigarettes and cheap meats. I was thinking about when we were small enough to run blind between what we thought was wheat and speckled wildflowers and I remembered the poor Bratz doll

one arm, hair hacked, green felt mono, that we buried a week after we returned from the dead up north, still haunted by the tears that ripped our parents' faces, we prepared our own funeral. We didn't know anything then. We were protected by witchcraft.

Several lengths of daisy chains. A palmful of Papatūānuku. A salt circle. Fake cries. Neither of us knew how to give eulogy so we sang the same old Māori songs twice. Trying on emotions the same way we tried on our mothers' makeup. Now the grass

is rarely neglected and if it was it would barely graze our waists. And we wear lipstick in ripe colours that our mothers never cared for. Now we can care for them in small ways, cut the fruit and feed our cousins. And the day it actually happens, we can always sing those songs.

My Mother Meets My Father in an Alternate Koru

I said fuck I feel Māori when I'm swimming in a river.
You looked at me with the sun escaping your grip.

In the river we look for pounamu or gold or
heart-shaped stones. I am hopeful.

I tell you what I live for.
Hot looks and hot summers.

You teach me how to cook an egg on a rock,
pick a big flat stone, carry the river in your hands
and watch if the water dances off.

I don't like eggs but I like you
I say come on
I'm trying to get a good look at your face.
Laugh for me babe, stick up the sun again.

When I look at you wading, the twist
in your waist is surprisingly delicate
and I can see the inheritance in you,
the ropes, your grandmother's jaw bone,
your hair so identical to your mother's
she must have wrapped you in it.

Then I think it would be good
for my children to have a father
like you cooking an egg on the rocks

watching the salt rise and reverse
back up to heaven.
Look

you say there are good things everywhere
you only have to train your eyes to look up.

A Karakia 4 a Humble Skux

I take a bath in my body of water
I take a bath in my body of water

I know I am the daughter of rangi papa tangaroa
I know I am the daughter of rangi papa tangaroa

& every yung god who fucked it up before me.
& every yung god who fucked it up before me.

Every day I breach the surface cleanly
Every day I breach the surface cleanly

& step out dripping so hard
& step out dripping so hard

ya better call a plumber.
ya better call a plumber.

God I'm a flex.
God I'm a flex.

I'm God's best sex.
I'm God's best sex.

I am made in the image of God.
I am made in the image of God.

I am made in the image of my mother.
I am made in the image of my mother.

I am made in the image of
I am made in the image of

my mountain
my river
my whenua.

my mountain
my river
my whenua.

Yeah I'm as fresh as my oldest tipuna.
Yeah I'm as fresh as my oldest tipuna.

Even when I'm lowkey I'm loud.
Even when I'm lowkey I'm loud.

Lil, but a million years old.
Lil, but a million years old.

I've been germinating like a seed
I've been germinating like a seed

been on my vibe like an atom
been on my vibe like an atom

& I am wilder than anything
& I am wilder than anything

my ancestors could have imagined.
my ancestors could have imagined.

So release the parts of me that call for change
So release the parts of me that call for change

but the energy is stale.
but the energy is stale.

I'm switching it all up
I'm switching it all up

fishing stars into the sea
fishing stars into the sea

and painting the skyful of whales.
and painting the skyful of whales.

Keep it humble, keep it skux.
Keep it humble, keep it skux.

Keep it pushing, keep it cute.
Keep it pushing, keep it cute.

I be in the marae doing the dishes
I be in the marae doing the dishes

cos there's mahi to do.
cos there's mahi to do.

Creator and Creation.
Creator and Creation.

I am made of the same
I am made of the same

star matter as legends.
star matter as legends.

Āmene.
Āmene.

Lesh go.
Lesh go.

My Ancestors Ride wit Me

My ancestors ride wit me.
They twerk on the roof of the Uber
as I'm pulling up late to the party.
They gas me full tank and
yas me in the mirror
as I summon them out of me with
my mascara wands and glitter and
every time I draw my eyes on
Nana you encourage me
to keep my chin lifted upwards,
my eyes filling up with stars.

I know I walk on
salt blood water tears.
I know the earth has been
beaten down and made gangsta
but sometimes, e hoas,
I just want to party

My ancestors ride wit me.
Don't tell me what they would do.
I know them better than you.

I sat in the lap of my great-grandmother
until the flax of her couldn't take it.
So she unravelled herself and
wrapped around me like a blanket
and at her touch the privilege of me
was a headrush as I remembered
making dresses out of sugar packets,

my bro getting blown up in Forlì,
my grandfather commemorated under one tree
even though he forced himself into our bloodline
and then abandoned me and me and me.
My mother saying go
marry a white man
you deserve better
so I left
the bone leftovers of home
knowing that in two generations I'd be called
an Oreo and my teeth painted into red brick,
two mouthfuls of red roots and boiling water
for dinner, for almost every dinner so
when I'm out with my mans eating
an expensive hunk of whatever
my ancestors and I share
the same taste and you can see it
in our smile so forceful it splits
the space–time continuum.
Weird flex I know. They taught me that
the entire universe is malleable and mine to mould.

Let me mould it in their image.

My ancestors ride wit me.
Don't you dare tell me what they would do.
I know them way better than you.

I've known them
since they were a five-year-old
who was told on her first day
she couldn't play because
she wasn't the right colour

but the other kids didn't know
that she was actually a witch,
a direct descendant
of tohunga and had
transformative powers
and in that instance
their hex became a spell
and it changed her into
an immortal thing,
a jaw, a whale, a knot
made from her grandmother's hair
and in that moment
she realised that life
was not going to be fair
but it could be
ferocious and forming
if she surrendered herself
to the brown, crying, clay.

She knew that one day
she would make something,
puoro, gourd, vessel, body
of water impossible enough
to carry them all.

My ancestors ride wit me.
Don't tell me wtf they would do.
I know them way better than you
and I know the wild
variety of things
they had to do
to get me here,
some voluntary,

some forced
not all of them
tika or textbook,
postcard or pretty,
but God!
Aren't you infatuated
with the nerve they had
to imagine me
and make it happen?
You can't tell me that
my existence isn't anything
but the existence of our old magic,
our old ways, our bloodlines,
our trust in the river,
when we first hopped in that
souped-up waka
& looked up at the stars like
u got me? & they said
hard
so now

I'm harder than a scrum of mountains.
I'm current like I'm water.
I whip like the wgtn wind and
I'm hotter than the sun.

And my ancestors ride wit me
like dawgs. When I whistle
they run and run and run.

ACKNOWLEDGMENTS

I want to acknowledge Ngāti Toa Rangatira, Ngāti Raukawa, and Te Āti Awa iwi for their whenua on which this book was written. I want to acknowledge Duvall Osteen, the team at Knopf, Amy, Linda, Simone, Matthew, and especially John Freeman for his support, time, and guidance but mostly for his friendship. I want to acknowledge the Native and Pacific Island communities for the endless mahi you do to create opportunities for Indigenous people to stand proud and protect what is sacred. I hope this offering helps connect our peoples past, present, and future. Thank you to SB.

A NOTE ON THE TYPE

This book was set in Scala, a typeface designed by the Dutch designer Martin Majoor (b. 1960) in 1988 and released by the Font-Font foundry in 1990. While designed as a fully modern family of fonts containing both a serif and a sans serif alphabet, Scala retains many refinements normally associated with traditional fonts.

Composed by North Market Street Graphics,
Lancaster, Pennsylvania

Printed and bound by Friesens,
Altona, Manitoba

Designed by Betty Lew